George Edward Jeans

**Haileybury chapel and other sermons**

George Edward Jeans

**Haileybury chapel and other sermons**

ISBN/EAN: 9783744744782

Printed in Europe, USA, Canada, Australia, Japan

Cover: Foto ©Lupo / pixelio.de

More available books at **www.hansebooks.com**

# HAILEYBURY CHAPEL

AND

## OTHER SERMONS

BY

The Rev. G. E. JEANS, M.A.

FELLOW OF HERTFORD COLLEGE, OXFORD

London

MACMILLAN AND CO.

1886

TO

### The Rev. Canon Bradby, D.D.,
LATE HEAD-MASTER OF HAILEYBURY:

UNDER WHOM I HAD THE PRIVILEGE OF SERVING FOR TEN YEARS AS ASSISTANT-MASTER OF THE SIXTH FORM, WITH EVER-GROWING RESPECT AND AFFECTION FOR HIM.

# HAILEYBURIA QUADRATA.

Reprinted from the *Haileyburian*, March 6, 1884, by permission of the Rev. J. Robertson, Head-Master of Haileybury College.

Four-square to all the winds that blow
  Are built the borders of our nest—
To sunny south and Zembla's snow,
  To rosy dawn and purple west:
So shall the banner of our pride
  For either fortune float unfurled,
To woo the breeze of summer-tide,
  Or breast the winters of the world!

The temple of our boyhood's home
  'Mid busy life embosomed lies;
Yet takes upon her stately dome
  The impress of the vaulted skies.
So may each trusty heart that here
  Fulfils his level course below,
Be rounded to the perfect sphere,
  Irradiant with ethereal glow.

O never be the memory drowned
  By manhood's strife or worldly care,
Of happy laughter ringing round
  Through all the fragrant summer air!
Of honest work and mimic wars,
  Of bosky heath and misty vale,
And holier thoughts beneath the stars
  To music of the nightingale.

                                 J. R.

> τὸν ἀγαθόν φασιν εἶναι τετράγωνον.
>
> ARISTOTLE, *Eth.* i.

QUATTUOR a ventis quot flant super aetheris axes
   stat bene quadrato limite nostra domus :
ille nives Boreae, terras hic spectat apricas,
   utque oriens rubeat sol, rutilusve cadat.
omine quo signum fortunam in utramque paratum
   inplendum ventis fortia corda dabunt ;
seu tenerum aestatis flatum captare licebit,
   seu rerum aspera hiems vincere si qua ferat.
   aedes stat medio veneranda, sed undique circum
   tot puerorum alto murmure mussat opus :
sed teres exsurgens camera tholus ille profunda
   prominet, inmensi parva figura poli.
tu quoque, fide puer, quod adest complere memento,
   munera quae tribuat sors tibi cumque die :
sic se quisque gerat totum teretemque, supernis
   vestiat ut radiis largior ille dies.
   o domus, ut numquam labor inprobus aut mala rerum
   nos cura inmemores suadeat esse tui !
risibus ut resonent omnes puerilibus agri,
   cum tepet aestivis suavior aura locis :
laeti opera ut pugnae cieant simulacra protervae,
   silva virens, vallis seu nebulosa iuvet ;
ipsa vel ut noctu subeat virtutis imago,
   voce sub astra animum cum Philomela vocat.

                                                         G. E. J.

# CONTENTS.

|   |   | PAGE |
|---|---|---|
| I. | HAILEYBURY CHAPEL, OR THE STONE OF WITNESS.—Joshua xxiv. 27 | 1 |
| II. | THE LIBERTY OF AN ENGLISH SCHOOL.—1 St. Peter ii. 16 | 21 |
| III. | SURSUM CORDA.—Acts i. 15 | 39 |
| IV. | CHRISTMAS.—St. Luke ii. 14 | 55 |
| V. | BIRDS-NESTING.—Deuteronomy xxii. 6, 7 | 73 |
| VI. | THE GREAT QUESTION.—St. Luke xviii. 8 | 91 |
| VII. | HEAVEN.—Zechariah viii. 5 | 109 |

# I.

## HAILEYBURY CHAPEL,

### OR THE STONE OF WITNESS.

(10th June 1883.)

*Almighty and everliving God, who hast vouchsafed to regenerate these thy servants by Water and the Holy Ghost, and hast given unto them forgiveness of all their sins: Strengthen them we beseech thee, O Lord, with the Holy Ghost the Comforter, and daily increase in them thy manifold gifts of grace; the spirit of wisdom and understanding; the spirit of counsel and ghostly strength; the spirit of knowledge and true godliness; and fill them, O Lord, with the spirit of thy holy fear, now and for ever. Amen.*

(From the ORDER OF CONFIRMATION.)

## Haileybury Chapel, or

"And Joshua said unto all the people, Behold, this stone shall be a witness unto us; for it hath heard all the words of the Lord which he spake unto us: it shall be therefore a witness unto you, lest ye deny your God."—JOSHUA xxiv. 27.

OF course the sermon this Sunday cannot but be about the Confirmation next Thursday. Week after week this term we have spent some part of the quiet Sunday in trying to make clear to the boys of our own houses the practical use as well as the duty of this rite: that for them a critical period of their school time is arrived, and that now, if ever, they must make themselves strong for the stress of the battle of life. Week after week have all the candidates come together one evening in the Chapel, to be reminded by their great numbers of the strength of union, and of the might of that army of God in which they are enrolling their name as recruits. And now, on the Sunday immediately preceding the Confirmation, the time is come for the preacher to sum up briefly what you have been taught, and to remind you what a solemn vow to God is contained in those two words : I DO.

I propose, then, to speak to you of the Book of Joshua ; not at all in the way in which you have it explained for the purpose of a Sunday lesson, but purely with this one object ; because the Book of Joshua might almost be edited as a Handbook to Confirmation. If this sounds strange, think of a few of the texts that crowd this book, and see how apt they are for you to remember next Thursday. For example, how God said to Joshua when

he began his work, "Be strong and of a
"good courage; be not afraid, neither be
"thou dismayed: for the Lord thy God
"is with thee whithersoever thou goest."[1]
Or how Joshua said to the tribes of Reuben
and Gad and half Manasseh when they
were going to leave the rest—just as many
of you will leave the rest this term—"Take
"diligent heed to love the Lord your God,
"and to walk in all his ways, and to keep
"his commandments, and to cleave unto
"him, and to serve him with all your heart
"and all your soul;"[2] and so Joshua
blessed them and sent them away. Or
how he said in his old age to all the people,
"If it seem evil unto you to serve the
"Lord, choose you this day whom ye will
"serve; but as for me and my house, we

---

[1] Josh. i. 9.  [2] Josh. xxii. 5.

"will serve the Lord."[1] Or lastly, think again of the words of my text, when the great stone of witness had been set up under the oak : "Behold, this stone shall "be a witness unto us; for it hath heard "all the words of the Lord which he "spake unto us : it shall be therefore a "witness unto you, lest ye deny your "God."[2]

Now, why is this so? Why is the Book of Joshua more than any other book of Bible history a *Confirmation* book? The answer is this—that the life which we live as individual human beings is reproduced in larger shape by masses of men living together as a nation or state. In other words, a nation, like a man, is born, is educated, grows to its strength, flourishes

[1] Josh. xxiv. 15.  [2] Josh. xxiv. 27.

awhile, begins to decline, and dies.[1] And the point which the Israelites had reached when we read about them in the Book of Joshua is precisely the point which you have reached to-day. For the nation was now awakening to a sense of its common manhood, and was about to be asked in all solemnity whether it would choose, or whether it would refuse, the service of God.

I will trace this more fully in the history of that wonderful nation to which the world owes so much. The nation of the Jews was born, we may say, when Jacob settled in Egypt. Then came the time of their childhood — a childhood carefully nursed so long as Joseph was there, but afterwards a very hard and bitter child-

---

[1] Compare Lucretius, ii. 73: *Augescunt aliae gentes, aliae minuuntur;* also Ov. Met., xv. 420.

hood, like that of a poor little street Arab, during the bondage in Egypt—when the people knew no more of the grand destiny in store for them than a child does whether he will be a famous man when he grows up, and when the principal lesson taught him is the lesson of simple *obedience*. Then arose their great lawgiver, Moses, who first awakened their intelligence by teaching them—just as you learn by coming to a great school—the consciousness of their being members of one body, and a body with immense capacities for doing noble things if they only had faith to do them. This done, he led them forty years through the wilderness, knowing nothing of where they were going, except that it was to a Promised Land. This was the early school time of the people. Then on the very edge of the Jordan their master is taken away from them, and the second great change takes place. A new leader they must have; but now he must be not merely a *master*, put over them they know not why, but a *leader* in the truest sense; one who will lead them by the divine right of his superiority, and whom they will follow to the death, because they believe in him.[1] This is where the Book of Joshua begins. The nation is now passing from its thoughtless boyhood to its early manhood; the stern battle for life on the other side of the river is coming very close; the obedience rendered must now be not a blind obedience, but a willing acceptance of duty to be done. Joshua therefore, rather than Moses, *confirms* them, so to speak, when he asks

[1] Compare the quotation in the note on p. 48.

them solemnly and openly either to choose or to refuse the service of God. What is all this but a type of your Confirmation?

But we may carry the parallel still further. What were the great duties of which Joshua reminded them? The first — for the order is unimportant — was utterly to put away all false gods. "Now "therefore," said he, "fear the Lord, and "serve him in sincerity and in truth: "and put away the gods which your "fathers served on the other side of the "flood, and in Egypt; and serve ye the "Lord."[1] The second was to believe in God's promises both of help and of punishment. "Ye know in all your hearts and "all your souls that not one good thing "hath failed of all the good things which

[1] Josh. xxiv. 14.

". the Lord spake concerning you. . . .
" Therefore it shall come to pass, that as
" all good things are come upon you, which
" the Lord promised you; so shall the
" Lord bring upon you evil things, when
" ye have transgressed the covenant of the
" Lord."[1] The third was that they should
keep the commandments of God. "Be
" ye therefore very courageous to keep and
" to do all that is written in the book of
" the law, that ye turn not aside therefrom
" to the right hand or the left."[2]

Now how very close a parallel this is to what the Bishop will say to you next Thursday. He will ask you whether, in God's presence, you will renew for yourselves the vow that was made for you when you were unconscious babies. And your

[1] Josh. xxiii. 14-16.     [2] Josh. xxiii. 6.

vow too, like theirs, was a threefold vow. It was, first, that you would put away all false gods: the worship of the selfishness, hollowness, and meanness of the world; the worship of those yet baser fleshly lusts which you have in common with the brutes; and above all the worship of that father of lies and of cruelty, the devil. It was, secondly, that whatever you knew to be the Word of God, that you would steadfastly believe. That you would believe in God the Father, who made you and loves you; in God the Son, who redeemed you by his sinless life and his willing death; and in God the Holy Spirit, who makes you holy too, because every noble thought we think and every noble deed we do comes straight from the influence of God. Thirdly, it was that since God wishes you not only to renounce what is bad but to choose what is good, you would keep his will and commandments, and walk in them all the days of your life. These are called the vow of Renunciation, the vow of Faith, and the vow of Obedience.

Once more, to complete this parallel, how closely the service that day at Shechem resembles what will be our service here. Joshua, as the minister of God, called the people together, and reminded them of the duties of renunciation, of faith, and of obedience; then he asked them solemnly to choose whether they would serve the many false gods or the one true God. And the people solemnly made answer, "We will serve the Lord." Then Joshua said, "Ye are witnesses against "yourselves that ye have chosen you the Lord, to serve him. And they answered, "We are witnesses." Then he took a great stone and set it up, perhaps in the very spot where Jacob long ago had worshipped,[1] that it might remind them for ever of the choice they had that day made, and so dismissed them. So, too, God's minister, the Bishop, will remind you of your baptismal vow of renunciation, of faith, and of obedience; he will then ask you solemnly to say whether, "in the presence of God and of this congregation," you renew this vow for yourselves at the time when life is opening out, and giving you the power to refuse the evil and choose the good. You will answer, I DO; and in that answer you will have

---

[1] Stanley: *Sinai and Palestine*, ch. v.

been witnesses against yourselves that you have chosen the Lord, to serve Him. Then that immemorial form of blessing, by which Joshua himself and the Bishop himself were ordained, will be administered to you by the laying on of hands; and so with the prayers of the Bishop, of your fathers and mothers, of those who have tried to guide you for this service, and not least, I trust, your own prayers that God will help you not to deny Him, you will be confirmed; and for good or evil—it must be one or the other—a great moment in your life will be over.

One thing, however, you may have noticed as wanting to our parallel. That is the ceremony of the *stone of witness;* the great stone which Joshua set up under an oak that was by the sanctuary of the

Lord;[1] so that when the people looked on it they might remember that day and the solemn choice they had made. What shall be our stone of witness?

It is of course true enough to say that our religion must be spiritual; that if it is to be worth anything it must be graven not on stone but on the fleshy tablets of the heart. That is true, I say, but it is not all. Signs and symbols have not lost, they never can lose, their power of recalling a fading thought or wandering memory, and of awakening into new life what seemed perhaps to have vanished away. Let, then, this beautiful Chapel itself, with its noble dome rising in the centre of our busy life[2]—built and

[1] Josh. xxiv. 26.
[2] See the poem, "Haileyburia Quadrata," at the beginning of the book.

decorated by the piety and loyalty of past and present Haileyburians—be for ever henceforth to you *the great stone of witness*; and among the many memories that will cluster in after days around it, keep sacred and inviolate the memory of the great oath you swore to God within its walls. Let it be a witness to you in the prayers you offer there henceforward. How often has the silent witness looked down on the ghastly mockery of a service that was not even lip-service; on rows of listless heads reclined on lounging elbows; on a dull vacancy where there should have been an echoing response; on God's house entered and left without one thought of God! Resolve that this at least, for all you who are to be confirmed, shall be so no longer. Think what a hundred and twenty newly-earnest voices scattered over the Chapel might do for this reproach, and then that mockery will be swept away, and the service will be no bond-service any longer, but a willing offering of prayer and praise, spreading its happy contagion of sympathy through the whole broad congregation.

Secondly, let it be a witness to you when you make your first Communion. For your Confirmation is a preparation for that great mystery; and next Sunday all of you will come for the first time with your elders to receive the Holy Sacrament. Assuredly you will come that first time with reverence and godly fear; but your fear will not be darkness; it will be the truest light. See, then, that you do not let this light grow dim. Make a vow then and there on your knees that you will come to that Sacrament regularly, humbly, and thankfully; not because it is customary or expected of you, but in the full spirit of what Jesus Christ meant when He said, "Do this in remembrance of me."

Lastly, let it be a stone of witness to you when you have crossed the river and begun the battle of life in earnest. At the end of this term a larger number than at other times will leave us; particularly among the prefects, with whom I personally have most to do in the work of the school; with some of whom I have, I trust, formed ties of lasting friendship; and some of whom I have prepared for their Confirmation. To you then, specially, my friends, as the last words I can say to you in your places from this pulpit, I repeat, let this be a stone of witness to you "lest ye deny your "God." For God can be denied, as He is fulfilled, "in many ways."[1] He may be denied by a coarse atheism, but that is not likely to happen to you. He may be denied in a much more subtle way—by a foolish blinking of the truth, by a mean acceptance of a false or low and unworthy idea of him. Most often God is denied, not formally but really, by forgetfulness of him, and putting him out of daily life as if he was only meant for Sundays. When therefore you think of the dear old school you have left, or when you come back to it as old Haileyburians, let the first sight or thought of the Chapel be to you a stone of witness, appealing to you whether you have honestly kept the vow you made of

---

[1] Tennyson: "The Passing of Arthur."

renunciation, of faith, and of obedience; and let it waken you as with the sound of a trumpet from that deadly forgetfulness in which our better lives are apt to moulder away. So shall it be no silent witness, rising to heaven to appeal against those who have denied their God, but the lofty pillar bearing a beacon light, which has lighted an army now strong and of good courage, as they began for themselves the battle of life, in the struggle to reach the Promised Land. And remember that

> "Eyes rekindling, and prayers,
> Follow your steps as ye go;
> Ye fill up the gaps in our files,
> Strengthen the wavering line,
> Stablish, continue our march,
> On to the bound of the waste,
> On to the City of God."[1]

[1] Matthew Arnold: "Rugby Chapel."

## II.

## THE LIBERTY OF AN ENGLISH SCHOOL.

(Third Sunday after Easter, 1881.)

*Almighty and everlasting God, by whose Spirit the whole body of the Church is governed and sanctified; Receive our supplications and prayers which we offer before thee for all estates of men in thy holy Church, that every member of the same in his vocation and ministry may truly and godly serve thee; through our Lord and Saviour Jesus Christ. Amen.*

(COLLECT FOR GOOD FRIDAY.)

"*As free, and not using your liberty for a cloak of maliciousness* [wickedness], *but as the servants of God.*"—1 St. Peter ii. 16.

We are very proud of our freedom as Englishmen, and so we ought to be; so proud of it that we would not merely fight for it—almost any nation would do that—but would always take care to keep it pure from the stain of anything slavish; and that is a far harder thing. The Romans too were rightly proud of their freedom. " With a great sum," said the chief captain to Paul, " obtained I this freedom." "But " I," proudly replied the Apostle, " was free " born."[1] Perhaps, however, of all people that have ever lived the proudest were the Jews. We know how for a long time they

[1] Acts xxii. 28. Compare the well-known passage of Cicero, Verr. v. 63.

had no king at all; how they were gradually forced into demanding one because of the obvious disadvantage of any division of power in an army; how they were cónquered and enslaved for a bitter time by the great kings of Babylon and Nineveh, but freed themselves at last from that yoke; and how, finally, like every other nation in the civilised world, they had to bow down before the irresistible might of Rome, from which yoke they could not escape till the Roman Empire itself began to fall to pieces. But they never submitted patiently, even when they had to submit. Every Jew thought it an intolerable hardship, to be resented on the very smallest chance of success; and the most violent sect, called the Zealots—who were like the Root and Branch men in our own Revolution—

thought it a positive sin against God to acknowledge any king who was not a Jew, or who derived his power from being a vassal of the Roman Emperor. Any adventurer, no matter how hopeless his chances were, who once set up the standard of revolt, was perfectly certain of a following; and hence it came about that the splendid toleration which the Romans showed for all other religions [1] was naturally put aside in the case of the Jews and the Christians, whom they regarded as being, from the strength of their faith, the most obstinate sect of the Jews. A Jewish Christian therefore had double cause for fear—the hatred of his race and the special hatred of his religion.

[1] See a fine example of this toleration in Cic. *Ad Fam.* iv. 12, with a note on the passage in my *Cicero's Life and Letters*, p. 323; and compare Farrar: *St. Paul*, ch. xxviii.

Now in the first verse of this epistle you will see that it is Christian Jews, scattered about in the different countries of Asia Minor, whom St. Peter was mainly addressing. And he knew very well the danger to which they might expose themselves by violent or even by incautious conduct; how the name of Christ might be dishonoured, and the position of Christians be made unsafe, if their liberty as Christians was wrongly used. As Christians they were free from the law of Moses,—well and good. But if that were taken to mean that they were free from the duties which the law had taught them, why then their boasted liberty was but a cloak of wickedness. As Christians they acknowledged Christ for their true King; but if that meant that they would deny the authority

of the Roman Emperor, or the King of Judæa, or the Governor of their own province, then they would rightly be regarded as pestilent rebels, who learnt their rebellion from their religion. It was the duty then of the Christian, and the birthright of his freedom, to live both a pure and a law-abiding life. "Dearly beloved," said the Apostle, "abstain from fleshly lusts,
" which war against the soul; making your
" life honourable among the Gentiles: that
" whereas they speak against you as evil-
" doers, they may when they see your good
" works glorify God."[1] And so the Christian freedom really comes to this, that the Christian binds himself hand and foot against everything that is wrong. He glories in submitting himself, just because

[1] 1 St. Peter ii. 11, 12.

he *is* free, to the law of God, and for God's sake also to the law of man; that he may not use his liberty for a cloak of wickedness, but as the bond-servant or slave of God.

Not merely the "servant" of God, as our version has it, but the bond-servant or slave—for St. Peter uses the stronger word. And indeed the word must have been a great deal stronger to people then than it can be to anybody now, who has never seen a slave in his life, but only read about them in *Uncle Tom's Cabin*. Think what the ordinary life of a slave in the Roman world was—the chattel of his master, just as much as a horse; and then think what a new life was made his by the preaching of these Apostles, when they told him, with that passionate faith that makes men believe, that he, the poor slave, had a soul to be saved, and one as dear in God's sight as the soul of his master. They told him that Jesus Christ, who was the only Son of God, had chosen willingly to make himself of no reputation, and take upon him the form of a slave, so that in him the divisions of Jew and Gentile, bondman and freeman, might be broken down, and all who let themselves be led by the Spirit of God might be the sons of God. That is why the early Christian churches were filled with slaves, and with the poorest and lowest classes of society; men who, if they had now been led by blind guides, would have revolted against the necessary foundations on which all ordered society must be built up—just as the Anabaptists, who said that Christ had set them free from all law, did in Westphalia and other parts of Germany in the sixteenth century. Had the Apostles given one moment's sanction to this; had they failed to insist sternly on the duty of the freeman to obey all lawful authority, the Christians would certainly, and not unjustly, have been condemned for their religion's sake, and Christianity would really have proved what Tacitus calls it in his famous sentence, *exitiabilis superstitio*,[1] "an accursed superstition." And when we consider the immense change in all habits of thought involved in this new teaching, that all men are equal in the sight of God—and that this teaching must be carried out without overthrowing a single foundation of law and order until some better foundation had been built in its

[1] *Ann.* xv. 44.

place—I venture to think that Christ was working through his Apostles just as real a *miracle*—though we do not generally call it so—as when he turned the water into wine, or fed the starving multitudes with bread. And the Apostles did this mainly by insisting that the Christian was free, not in order that he might escape from the law, but that he might make himself all the more willingly and absolutely the servant of God.

Now let us apply this to ourselves. We are proud—and again rightly proud—of the wide liberty given in English public schools—a liberty which excites the amazement as well as envy of every foreign observer.[1] We ought to be proud of it—

---

[1] Striking testimony to this is borne by a French master in England, M. Max O'Rell, both in *John Bull et son île* and in *Les chers voisins*.

so proud as to feel that this liberty is a tie much more binding than any number of *pions* or ushers spying about could possibly be. And then again this freedom is wisely made not invariable, but of a kind that grows with our growth. More trust is reposed in a boy of higher than in one of lower position; far more still in a prefect, that he may learn the rightful use of authority. Now to all honourable minds a greater trust always brings a greater sense of obligation with it, and this is the true force of the really grand old maxim, *noblesse oblige.* I know it has frequently been the case that a boy who has been in the habit of breaking certain rules while in the Fifth Form, has felt that he cannot do so any longer when he becomes a prefect. And why? Because he is more watched in his higher position? No, it is just the contrary; it is because this very trusting has awakened his sense of duty in his position; because the truer sense of his real freedom has made him feel it a shame that his liberty should only be "a cloak of wicked-"ness."

And if this feeling is right and honourable, and what you would yourselves feel to be essential for any prefect you would respect, you must remember, my friends, that the same thing applies—in its degree—to every one of you. If you forget this, and show one face when a master is there and another when he is away; if you scamp your work or cut it down to the minimum of time because you are in a study instead of a form-room; if you misspend some time entrusted to you for use because you will probably not be detected; then you might perhaps make a tolerable slave under a task-master's eye, but you are helping to discredit an English public school and its noble traditions of freedom, and you are making yourself unfitted to be hereafter a loyal citizen of that free country of whose liberty you would loudly maintain you are so proud.

You see, then, that this strange thing is true, that the only way to be really free is to obey the right with absolute obedience; and that the more entirely unbreakable rules we acknowledge, so long as the rules are right, the freer and happier we are. I will therefore add a word on the four little rules for a free Christian which St. Peter gives in the Epistle for to-day, and so will end. They are these: " Honour all men. Love "the brotherhood. Fear God. Honour the king."[1] *Fear God* first, for that is the beginning of wisdom.[2] "I will walk at liberty," says the writer of the 119th Psalm; and why? Because I do my own will? No, but "because I seek thy commandments."[3] *Honour the king* as representing all constituted authority in your own country: not with any slavish veneration for the king's person, still less for the king's family or surroundings, which is degrading to a free man, but with that loyal respect to all true authority, whether of king or governor, bishop or magistrate, father or schoolmaster, which true self-respect not only does not forbid but demands. *Honour all men.* For that self-respect which comes with the con-

---

[1] 1 St. Peter ii. 17.    [2] Prov. ix. 10.    [3] Ps. cxix. 45.

sciousness of freedom, so far from taking away, gives us a new sense of respect for others. Be courteous and considerate to all who are in a lower station than yourself, and do all you can to keep up, not to degrade, that self-respect in them which is their best hope for elevating themselves. There is no man, however low, but is in some sense worthy of honour when we remember that for that poor creature, whether a savage of Central Africa or a savage of London streets, Jesus Christ was not too high to take the form of a slave and to die. And lastly, *love the brotherhood*, "for "we are all members one of another."[1] "Do good unto all men,"[2] first, if you will, to those who are of the house-

---

[1] Rom. xii. 5.     [2] Gal. vi. 10.

hold of faith, but still unto all men, for they are our brothers. For nearly two thousand years we have been slowly growing in the perception of this. We now acknowledge the rights of weak or savage nations in a way that would have seemed foolish or dangerous to an advanced philosopher a century ago. We now keep on giving more power to the poorest class, in a way that would be certain destruction to the state were it not for the growing sympathy and understanding, thank God, between class and class, and in that sympathy is our security. This is how it is that Christ has changed and is changing the whole social condition of the world, without overthrowing—indeed making far stronger—the security and peace in which we live; by showing that the free man is the most obedient to good laws, and that his very freedom makes him all the more fear God, honour the authority which comes from God,[1] honour all men because in God's sight they are as himself, and love all men, because they are his brothers, for whom Christ died.

[1] Rom. xiii. 1.

## III.

## SURSUM CORDA.

(Sunday after Ascension, 1880.)

*Grant, we beseech Thee, Almighty God, that like as we do believe thy only-begotten Son our Lord Jesus Christ to have ascended into the heavens; so we may also in heart and mind thither ascend and with him continually dwell, who liveth and reigneth with thee and the Holy Ghost, one God, world without end. Amen.*

(Collect for Ascension Day.)

"*Why stand ye gazing up into heaven?*"—ACTS i. 15.

ASCENSION DAY is past again, and you have already had it pointed out to you that the obvious lesson to be learnt from the day is one that should appeal rather specially to us Haileyburians, being the same as that noble motto for a public school—"SURSUM CORDA," "Lift up your hearts"—that meets the eye above our gate, and is blazoned in colours on the west wall of our Chapel. But on this day, which naturally belongs to the same season, I wish to add a thought as a supplement, which may seem at first sight to contradict, but is really necessary to the other.

For is not this text of mine, though it comes from the Epistle for Ascension Day, almost a contradiction to the special teaching of the day? "If ye be risen with "Christ," said St. Paul, "seek those things "that are above, where Christ is seated on "the right hand of God."[1] But what else were the disciples doing when the angels rebuked them for standing gazing into heaven, as though they would bid them turn from heaven to earth?

And so they did bid them. It was not rapture, even of the most holy kind, but *work* that their Master wanted of them now. The bright vision had passed into heaven and gone; and now were coming the stern realities that the Christian faith meant then — the hard life of thankless labour, ending perhaps by the sword or the faggot. But did not St. Paul know this too when he wrote those words

[1] Col. iii. 1.

amongst his weariness and painfulness, his watchings often, and daily care of all the churches? Surely no man ever knew it better than the greatest of all the Apostles.

Here then you have the contrast between the two principles of Christian life which I wanted you to mark—one, that we must seek those things that are above, where Christ is at the right hand of God; the other, that we are called upon not to gaze into heaven, but to work for God upon earth. In other words, unless we form in our own minds a very noble idea of what our conduct should be, we shall never be likely to do a noble action at all; then even the very noblest ideas are of no value whatever, except in so far as they lead to action or help to shape our lives. But if those noble thoughts and wishes are real and not affected, if they are full of desire to help others, not merely to save ourselves, then they will shape the life even of a child.

Not long ago I was on the bridge that leads out of the Great Gate at Avila in Spain—a wonderful old town, with walls far more perfect than our own Chester, which looks as if nothing but the railway station there was not of the Middle Ages—and there I thought of telling you something of the story of St. Theresa. St. Theresa lived at Avila about the middle of the sixteenth century. Now she and her little brother used to read together the lives of the saints and martyrs, until they desired that they too might win the glorious crown. She was but seven or eight, and her little brother younger still, when they started across that bridge one morning from Avila in order to go to the Moors, who were Mohammedans, and then held the south of Spain, in order to tell them that they loved Jesus Christ, in the hope that then they would be murdered and so go straight to heaven. Poor little creatures! Of course they were soon found and brought back, and so their child's story ended. But though that story ended, St. Theresa never forgot the idea which shaped her beautiful life. When she grew up she reformed the Order of the Carmelites, diffused a new earnestness through all the Spanish Church, and did for a time in Spain much of the best that the Reformation was doing in Germany and England. She is one of the most venerated of the saints, and in Spanish pictures you may see her with an arrow tipped with the flame of zeal, while at her ear is a pure white dove, signifying the Holy Spirit of God that moulded her pure and holy life.

But remember that in the sight of God the life of St. Theresa would have been just as pure and as noble if she had succeeded in doing nothing at all of these things, but had only tried her best, and been forced to confess that it was a failure. "Here and there," as George Eliot says, "a cygnet is reared uneasily among the "ducklings in the brown pond, and never "finds the living stream in fellowship with "its own oary-footed kind. Here and "there is born a Saint Theresa, foundress "of nothing, whose loving heart-beats "and sobs after an unattained goodness tremble off and are dispersed among hindrances, instead of centering in some long recognisable deed."[1]

Yes, thank God, every one of us has his better moments, such as they are; the better moments are not given to the saints alone — only the true saint seizes on the better moment and makes it a part of his life. Surely I may safely say there is not one of us who does not at times feel something stirring within him that makes him wish that he was good—that he was leading a better life altogether than he is leading. It may be from his Confirmation; it may be from a letter from home; or because some one whom he loved dearly has been laid in the grave; or it may seem to be

---

[1] Prelude to *Middlemarch*.

without any reason, as if God had shot a chance arrow into the air. But I appeal to you all without fear — has not every one of you felt a longing at times, and found himself the better for so feeling, that he too could do something for the honour of God or to smite the devil—at least that it might be said of him afterwards that he had been a manly, pure, and honourable English boy, and that even a great English public school was all the better because he had once been a member of it? Well, if you have ever felt anything of that kind, you too have been "*seeking those things which are above;*" and though you will never reach all that you wish or pray for, that idea of goodness, like a star in the heavens, has attracted your life in the little world below, as the distant moon silently attracts each little wave of the sea.[1]

Do not think that a preacher is talking above your heads if he urges you to think of something infinitely noble as what you must aim at; something as far above the life even of a saint as a star is above the ground. There is no fear here of fixing your thoughts so high that you may perhaps miss your mark altogether. Always bear in mind George Herbert's famous lines—

> "Pitch thy behaviour low, thy projects high,
>   So shalt thou humble and magnanimous be;
> Sink not in spirit; who aimeth at the sky
>   Shoots higher much than he that means a tree."[2]

---

[1] "Surely whoever speaks to me in the right voice
Him or her I shall follow:
As the water follows the moon silently
With fluid steps anywhere around the globe."
WALT WHITMAN, quoted in *Daniel Deronda*, ch. 29.

[2] "The Church Porch."

If the highest ideal that a boy has put to himself is to get his form prize this term, or to get his eleven-colours, and he succeeds in this object, well, he *has* done a good thing as far as it goes; but he has not mounted half so high for all his success as the boy who has said, "God helping " me I will try to stop a wicked thing," and has tried to stop it, and then has failed or been laughed at. That is because one *aims at the sky*, whereas the other only *meant a tree*.

Lastly, I wish to say a few words specially addressed to the elder ones of you in the Sixth Form. Most of you will be leaving us at the end of this term to go to Oxford or Cambridge, or into the army, or to an hospital, or into business. Wherever it is, you must of course take a plunge into different ways of thinking from what you have been used to, and most of you will be quite sure to be carried away for a time by any popular tendency; and the popular tendency is now (I suppose it always has been) to prevent anybody from ever setting his eyes on any lofty ideal at all. Perhaps I may venture here to quote from a lay-sermon delivered at Clifton College by a warm friend of Haileybury, the well-known author of *Tom Brown's Schooldays.* Mr. Hughes very truly says, "If you have " not already felt it, you will assuredly feel " as soon as you leave these walls that your " lot is cast in a world which longs for no- " thing so much as to succeed in shaking " off all belief in anything which can- " not be tested by the senses, and gauged " and measured by the intellect, as the

" trappings of a worn-out superstition. . . .
" So the high priests of the new gospel
" teach, and their teaching echoes through
" our literature and colours the life of the
" streets and the markets in a thousand
" ways; and a Mammon-ridden generation,
" longing to be rid of what they hope are
" only certain old and clumsy superstitions
" —which they *try* to believe injurious to
" others, and are quite sure to make them
" uneasy in their own efforts to eat, drink,
" and be merry—applauds as openly as
" it dare, and hopes soon to see the mil-
" lennium of the flesh-pots publicly declared
" and recognised."[1]

Now, what I have to say to you is this. When you have to make your choice, take

---

[1] *The Manliness of Christ*, p. 175. I should like to see this admirable address circulated separately in all our great schools.

your stand modestly, but boldly and firmly, on the side which offers you not the safest or most popular but the noblest ideal of life. Do not let your attitude to what you have been taught to believe, if it is really noble, be one of half-hearted apology for it, as if it did not matter very much after all what people believed, and that the one thing needful is, not to be very different from other people.

But even in those special tendencies of our age which you often hear so bitterly denounced there seems to be a hopeful side. If it is true that we are often " Mammon-ridden "—that there is a going to and fro and hasting to be rich—that is an accompaniment of a vast extension of powers that may be used for good through all the human race. If there is incessant and uneasy searching into everything, and often a coarse and vulgar handling of some ark that holds what we deem sacred, yet that is an outward sign of the growing hatred of merely accepting a tradition, and of a desire to find out truth at any risk. Certainly this at least may be said for our age, that at no previous period in all history has the sympathy for suffering, or poverty, or weakness been so widely spread as it is now. It may be that Christianity will have to put off, perhaps with a violent effort, much that has been believed to be of it, but is not really of the Spirit of Christ. It may be that we are, as some think, on the verge of a great revolution of thought. If that be so, it will but appear all the more plainly why the ideal that Christ has set up for us stands so serenely far above all the possible changes and chances of this mortal life, and that he who lifts up his eyes to the everlasting hills will find that from them comes his help.[1]

Thus the strange truth that Christ sets up before us an impossible standard of life to follow is explained, because each step of the way is possible in itself. "Who shall "ascend into the hill of the Lord? who "shall rise up in his holy place? Even he "that hath clean hands and a pure heart."[2] For in the fine words of Emerson, which are written up in the Hall of Marlborough College—

> "So close is glory to our dust,
> So near is God to man,
> When duty whispers low, Thou must,
> The youth replies, I can."

[1] Ps. cxxi. 1.      [2] Ps. xxiv. 3, 4.

## IV.

## CHRISTMAS.[1]

(Third Sunday in Advent, 1879.)

*O Lord, who has taught us that all our doings without charity are nothing worth; Send thy Holy Ghost, and pour into our hearts that most excellent gift of charity, the very bond of peace and of all virtues, without which whosoever liveth is counted dead before thee; Grant this for Thine only Son Jesus Christ's sake. Amen.*

(COLLECT FOR QUINQUAGESIMA SUNDAY.)

---

[1] The idea of this sermon was partly suggested by two of Charles Kingsley's—A *Preparation for Christmas* and *Christmas Day*.

> "**Glory to God in the highest,
> And on earth peace, good will toward men.**"[1]
>
> St. Luke ii. 14.

CHRISTMAS is coming very soon now. There are many things that remind us of this. The ground is white with snow, and the ponds are beginning to be frozen hard; the shops are putting out their brightest show, and all of us have talked of what we shall do in the Christmas holidays. Before many days we shall all be in our own churches for the Christmas morning

---

[1] In this sermon I pointed out that the reading of four of the oldest MSS. of the Gospel was εὐδοκίας, not εὐδοκία,—not "peace, good will towards men," but "peace to men of [God's] good will;" and so also in the Vulgate, or version of St. Jerome, "*Pax hominibus bonae voluntatis.*" This has now been made familiar to every one by the Revised Version, "Peace among men in whom "he is well pleased." The Authorised Version however, which is strongly supported in the *Speaker's Commentary*, is so associated with Christmas texts that it seems better (with this note) to retain it here.

service; and there among the bright and pleasant decorations for the day we shall be sure to see the special Christmas text, "On earth peace, good will toward men." Therefore, as we never have the opportunity of saying a Christmas word to you here in this Chapel, I take this text a little before its season, in the hope that I may give you something fresh to think about it when you see or hear it on Christmas morning, and that this may help to make all the merrier for others as well as yourselves the Christmas holidays to which we are looking forward.

Have you ever thought why we keep Christmas as we do?—why we decorate our churches, and give presents to one another, and let our servants have a holiday if we can, and feel that it is a shame to let a quarrel run over Christmas Day? I suppose you would say, "Because Christ "was born on Christmas Day," or, "We "keep it so because we are Christians." Here then I must answer,—though it may seem a startling thing to say,—that, first, so far as we can discover, Christ was *not* born on Christmas Day; and secondly, that we should now have been keeping our festival apparently in just the same way if we had been Pagans still and not Christians.

As to the first, it is hardly possible that Jesus Christ can have been born on the 25th of December. In the verse before our text we read how the shepherds were "abiding in the field, keeping watch over "their flocks by night." Now, even in

Palestine, it would be very difficult for shepherds to remain out in the fields on a December night, and what is more, there would not have been any pasture for the sheep. Hence another fancy arose, but equally without any ground for it, that Christ was born on the early morning of the 5th of April—that being the day on which thirty-three years afterwards he died on the Cross. But it certainly was very early that the Christians began to keep their festival of the Saviour's coming, either at the end of the old year, or joined with the Epiphany at the beginning of the new; and since it is quite impossible to find out with certainty what the real time of the year was, we may at once agree that it was a singularly appropriate time to have chosen.

For with almost all the nations of the world that time was a fitting time of rejoicing already. The labours of the old year were done, and the labourers were resting before beginning the round afresh for the new year. The earth too takes her rest at this season, and lies asleep under her covering of snow, so that all the seeds may be matured in her bosom and burst into life when the spring is come. Therefore it was at Christmas time that the Romans kept the great festival of their god Saturn, the god of the seed hidden in the earth, just as the Norsemen then kept the festival of Yule-tide to the bountiful goddess Freya. So the end of the year all over the world was felt to be a fit time of rejoicing; and Christians naturally wished to join in the rejoicing too, but not in honour of those gods whom the heathen world were worshipping, but in honour of the baby who had been born at Bethlehem, and cradled there in the lowly manger, and yet was the Saviour of whom all the prophets had spoken, the promised Prince of Peace. This, and not any proof that existed, is the real reason why for so many hundreds of years we have kept our Christmas Day on the 25th of December.

Then again, do you say, we keep Christmas as we do because we are Christians? In a certain sense that is true, or it would not be a Christian festival at all. But it seems probable that we should have been doing very much what we are doing now if we had never heard of the name of Jesus Christ at all. Let us suppose that we were put down suddenly in the middle of Rome before Christ was born, and that the day of the year was the day on which we shall go home. It would then have been the second day of the great festival of the Saturnalia of which I was speaking. All the shops and the law-courts would have been shut, and it would have been holiday-time in the schools. The streets would have been full of people going about with presents to one another for a Happy New Year;[1] and if it was evening you would see maskers and mummers going to play in great houses; and a favourite amusement was carrying wax tapers, the fun being to keep your own taper alight and blow out other people's, just as they

[1] They were called *strenae*, from which comes the French *étrennes*.

do in Rome now on the last night of the Carnival.¹ To begin a war then would have been thought quite impious. Even the poor criminals in prison were never tortured or executed then, but had their punishment made a little lighter. But the most curious custom of all was that, just for that once, the slaves were recognised as human creatures, and allowed to play at being free.² They were allowed to dress up in their masters' or mistresses' clothes, and sat down to a feast in the evening where their masters and mistresses waited on them; and a very good as well as pretty custom this was, because it must have done something to keep alive in a

---

[1] See Dickens: *Pictures from Italy—Rome.*
[2] "Age, libertate Decembri,
Quando ita maiores voluerunt, utere."
Hor., *Sat.* ii. 7, 5.

Roman's heart what he was only too ready always to forget, that his slave was a human being after all.

Well then, if we found ourselves suddenly one winter in the midst of this we should fancy that people were keeping Christmas. So, perhaps, in a way they were, for St. Paul says, " God in times past " suffered the nations to walk in their own " ways. Nevertheless he left not himself " without witness, in doing us good and fill- " ing our hearts with food and gladness." [1] Perhaps it was so with these Romans. Those who had worked hard were enjoying their holiday, and that is a good thing. They were expressing their thankfulness to the god who, as they believed, had given them their seedtime, and that also

[1] Acts xiv. 16, 17.

is good; but better still was the kindness of friends and relations to one another, which was shown by these little presents, and the meeting again of families for the festival season, and the stopping of all quarrels, whether with the sword or in the law-courts, for the time, and the sympathy for once of masters and mistresses with their poor slaves; all of which did tell the Romans before Christ came something of Christ's good tidings of peace on earth and good will towards men.

When therefore you see this text up in church next Christmas morning remember that though this was no new Gospel, the blessedness of peace and good will, yet that it was Christ's coming which made this the living principle of the Christian life. Think of this in reference to those things which we generally associate with Christmas time. You will, no doubt, be giving little presents to friends and relations, and receiving others from them. Well, and so did the Romans, you see, before Christ was born; but it is quite a new thing that the thoughtfulness and love implied in each present should be really for the sake of Him who loved us so much. Again, it is a time when we naturally feel that quarrels and bitter feelings should at least be put aside, and so thought the Romans when they stopped their lawsuits and their battles; but it is the part of a Christian not only to hush for the time but to heal altogether whatever he can of any quarrelling or unkindness that may have arisen in the past year, and to do it for the sake of the Divine Forgiver of injuries.

Again, it is a time when you can do something towards breaking down that inhuman separation of classes that is perhaps worse in free England than in any other country. The Romans, we see, did it a little in an odd way at their Saturnalia, but you can all do much more. Most of you live in country villages, and there it is far the easiest. You can always, to begin with, show a human interest in your own servants at home, and be careful about hurting their feelings, or glad to help them, if occasion arises, by a little sacrifice of your own convenience. You can go about in the village, and get to know something about poor people, and see what a hard life and yet what a patient life they often lead; and the mere knowing of it will do both you and them good. Poor people often say that the mere sight of a bright face does them good; and if you are giving up half an hour, when you might have been skating, to read the Bible to a poor bedridden creature, or giving a little present—out of your own money—to help a poor woman who is struggling to keep out of the workhouse, or even only giving a few kind words—and meaning them—to the people with whom you have to do, then you are helping to spread the message of Jesus Christ.

Lastly, you will have everything at Christmas to remind you of all this, if you only care to think about it at all. Here is a beautiful description of a Christmas morning walk from the great and tender-hearted novelist, who has done more than all the philosophers put together to spread kindly

feeling for the poor, and to break down those inhuman barriers of which I was speaking. "And now," he says, "the
" mists began to rise in the most beautiful
" manner, and the sun to shine; and as I
" went on through the bracing air, seeing
" the hoar-frost sparkle everywhere, I felt
" as if all nature shared in the joy of the
" great Birthday. Going through the
" woods the softness of my tread upon
" the mossy ground and among the brown
" leaves enhanced the Christmas sacred-
" ness by which I felt surrounded. As the
" whitened stems environed me I thought
" how the Founder of the time had never
" raised his benignant hand save to bless
" and heal, except in the case of one un-
" conscious tree. I came to the village,
" and the churchyard where the dead had

"been quietly buried in the sure and cer-
"tain hope which Christmas time inspired.
"What children could I see at play and
"not be loving of, recalling who had loved
"them? . . . In time the distant river
"with the ships came full in view, and
"with it pictures of the poor fishermen
"mending their nets, who rose and fol-
"lowed him—of the teaching of the people
"from a ship pushed off a little way from
"the shore, by reason of the multitude—
"of a majestic figure walking on the water
"in the loneliness of the night. My very
"shadow on the ground was eloquent of
"Christmas; for did not the people lay
"their sick where the mere shadows of
"the men who had heard and seen him
"might fall as they passed along?"[1]

[1] Dickens: *The Seven Poor Travellers.*

Keep, then, something of these thoughts to make these Christmas holidays happy, and remember that one of the best ways to give glory to God in the highest is to help on earth peace, good will towards men.

## V.

## BIRDS-NESTING.

(May 1885.)

*O God, forasmuch as without thee we are not able to please thee: mercifully grant that thy Holy Spirit may in all things direct and rule our hearts: through Jesus Christ our Lord. Amen.*

(Collect for 19th Sunday after Trinity.)

"If a bird's nest chance to be before thee in the way in any tree, or on the ground, whether they be young ones, or eggs, and the dam sitting upon the young, or upon the eggs, thou shalt not take the dam with the young: But thou shalt in any wise let the dam go, and take the young to thee; that it may be well with thee, and that thou mayest prolong thy days."
—Deut. xxii. 6, 7.

I SUPPOSE hardly any of you ever heard a sermon on birds-nesting, and probably it is a surprise to find that there really is a text in the Bible speaking quite plainly about birds-nesting and about nothing else. As the subject then is not too small for the Bible to notice, it cannot be too small for us; and as it is part of a subject on which I feel very strongly indeed—the love of and care for God's creatures—I should like to speak of it to you in this summer season, with the birds nesting in every bush around us, or their newly taken eggs displayed in everybody's collection.

The first thing we may notice is that, not only does it seem surprising to find a positive command on so small a subject, but that the circumstances under which the command was delivered were—as far as we can find out—such as to make this more surprising than ever. That wonderful people, the Israelites, had not long before been made into a nation at all instead of a mere crowd of slaves, owing to the commanding genius of Moses, one of the grandest figures in all history, whom God raised up for this special work. Under his command they wandered for many long years in the wilderness, slowly working their way towards the Land of

Promise. At last came the time when their great leader was to be taken from them, just when that land was in sight, and when it seemed that under proper guidance a happy settlement was about to begin for the people he had loved and led so well. This then is the professed occasion of the Book Deuteronomy, or the Second Recital of the Law — though the actual date of the work is a disputed point — the last solemn charge of the great father of his people; the last reminder of the sure punishment of sinning against God, and His equally sure blessing upon obedience to His commandments.

Yes, obedience: but not obedience for its own sake, which is no virtue at all in a reasoning being, but obedience to God's commandments, because they are always good. The Jewish scribes, being mostly quite incapable of entering into the spirit instead of the letter of their law, used to say that this was the very least among the commandments of Moses; and sermons have been preached on this text to show that God likes commanding us to do little things in order to put our obedience to the proof; and that it is a higher thing to obey God in something for which there is no reason except that God so ordered it, than to obey in some great thing, such as, *Thou shalt do no murder*, which the laws of nature might teach us without any revelation at all.[1]

Now this is exactly the view which I

---

[1] Canon Melvill, the famous preacher, after whom Melvill House is named, has a fine and suggestive sermon on this text (*Sermons on the less Prominent Facts of the Bible*, vol. ii.), in which, nevertheless, he uses this deplorable argument.

want you at once to reject, as dishonouring alike to God and man, both in this and in any other commandment of the Bible. If you glance at the Books of Exodus or Deuteronomy you may find scores of commandments which perhaps seem trifling or even absurd, if you want to find anything absurd in them. But if you ask a special student of these books and of that age, he will tell you that while some of these commandments are not yet satisfactorily explained, still, that every year adds to our knowledge on the point: that some of these seemingly mysterious directions are really wise rules about health, adapted to the climate; some are explained by the idolatrous ritual of the Egyptians or the tribes of Canaan, which was to be carefully avoided; others probably bear in their form the stamp of the personality of the great lawgiver himself. But whether any particular command is fully explained or not, this we may, at any rate, assert as a principle to begin with: that a law is not good because it is God's, but that God has made it His law because it is good.

I will not, however, lead you any farther into this general question, but will at once ask—*Why* does the Bible say if a bird be sitting on her young, or eggs, that we must not take the mother-bird even if we take her young?

And here it may perhaps help us if I quote by way of illustration a very curious parallel that may be found in a poet called Phocylides, who lived at least a thousand years later than Moses. He was a Greek of the great Ionic race living in

Asia Minor—the race that was then at the head of all the culture and civilisation in the world. Now he wrote what is called didactic poetry; that is to say, useful maxims or proverbs in verse; and he happened by chance to lay down a rule of advice on the very same subject as our text. And this is what he says—

> "Let no one take all the birds of a nest together;
> But leave the mother, that you may have her young a second time."[1]

The Greek poet therefore says, "Leave "the mother alone, because thus you have "a chance of destroying her home and her "young a second time." Moses says, "If

---

[1] μηδέ τις ὄρνιθας καλιῆς ἅμα πάντας ἑλέσθω,
μήτερα δ' ἐκπρολίπῃς ἵν' ἔχῃς πάλι τῆσδε νεοσσούς.
There is great doubt as to the genuineness of the fragments of Phocylides, but the question is not worth discussion here, since they undoubtedly express the sentiments of his time.

"you are taking young birds, spare the mother at least if you wish God to bless you." You could not possibly have a better example how the words of the great lawgiver lift one into a totally different sphere of thought from the wisest maxims of the ancient world.

For why is it that the mother-bird, sitting on her nest, is in any danger at all more than the father, or than she herself is at other times when she has no nest? Clearly, because of the sweet instinct which God has given her, to protect her young by any means in her power. You know how a cat with kittens will rout any dog; how a hen with chickens has even beaten off a kite or killed a large rat; how a lapwing, not being able to fight, will pretend to have a broken wing to draw you away from her nest. And so it is just the nobility of this beautiful instinct which puts the brave little mother in danger, while the father-bird gets safely away. If you have a gentle hand you may stroke some of the tamer birds, such as a thrush or a robin, on their nests; but what manliness or generosity must a boy have who would make use of this brave instinct to capture the poor bird for a cage as well as take her nest? We may perhaps remember some other remarkable commandments which nature and humanity approve of, such as not to kill a cow and her young in the same day,[1] and not to seethe a kid in its mother's milk.[2]

And then again the concluding sentence of the text, " that it may be well with thee,

---

[1] Lev. xxii. 28.    [2] Exod. xxiii. 19.

" and that thou mayest prolong thy days," points us clearly to the true ground for this commandment. One of the ten commandments, and one only, expressly called therefore "the first commandment with "promise,"[1] has the very same sentence added to it as a sanction. "Honour thy "father and thy mother, that thy days may "be long in the land which the Lord thy "God giveth thee." This is surely intentional; it was surely intended that we should see not only that here was a plain rule, but that the rule was good in itself: that not amongst men, but amongst animals also the affection of a mother for her young is a sacred gift of God; and that to violate this, or even to run the risk of weakening it by making it a fresh source of

[1] Ephes. vi. 2.

danger, is to violate the best instincts in our own nature, and so to offend against the laws of God.

Now if it should seem to you that, if this be so, we have no right to take a bird's eggs at all, I reply that if you really feel scruples about it you had certainly much better not take eggs. But most of you will not feel scruples, and to you I can say that our text seems to give us the wise, moderate, and humane rule. Look at the text again : "Thou shalt in any wise "let the dam go, and take the young to "thee." For God has given all living creatures into the hand of man, only they are for our use and not for abuse. The bird's eggs, and even the bird's young ones if we require them, are ours, whether we want them for food, or for the study of natural history, or merely for the genuine love of their beauty; but, whatever our object, we have to remember that no cruelty to God's creatures is so small as to go unnoticed in God's sight. There is no real cruelty, happily, in proper birds-nesting, nothing which we have not a perfect right to do, if only we remember this. And I as one who have collected and delighted in birds' eggs since I was much younger than any of you here, and have helped the collections of so many Haileybury boys, can emphatically assert that the cruelty hardly ever comes from the true collector, the lover of birds and their ways, but from poor ignorant boys who have never learnt to think about birds as God's creatures, or from those much more blamable boys here who thoughtlessly encourage their mischief. Here then is a plain, easy way of keeping the spirit of this commandment. You know, for example, how the poor boys round here always pull out a nest bodily in order to make a few pence out of you; but you, who by buying of them encourage this cruel mischief, will have to answer for it far more than they. Put down then as low and cruel this tearing out of nests to make money, this plundering of a whole nest instead of an egg or two: remember that with the gentleness and care which a good collector always uses, few birds need ever be forced to desert their nests; and bear in mind the difference between taking eggs (which to the bird, after all, only means some labour spent in vain) and taking young birds, for whom the poor little mother has the same affection in kind, though not in degree, as our mothers have for you and me.

No; you need not be afraid that a love of natural history, or the thoughtful and careful collection of its specimens, will ever make you more cruel, or increase in the end the misery that so many dumb animals are doomed to. On the contrary, I hold that this, better than anything else, teaches us that sympathy with God's creation which is the best safeguard against thoughtless cruelty; for a true naturalist is always tender-hearted. We think of Gilbert White, the delightful parson of Selborne, who has first taught so many to love the simple country, and how he delighted in the honey-buzzard's egg on Selborne Hanger; or Waterton, and his walled park in which the birds became as tame as in an aviary; or Thomas Edward, the wonderful Scotch shoemaker-naturalist, who spent whole nights in the woods to watch the badgers and stoats, and how he went up to the high roof for a sparrow's nest when he was a mere baby, but cried when he was a big boy over the fate of the little sparrow he had even trained to do tricks; or Frank Buckland, whose charming Life has just been published, and who said on his deathbed, " God is so good, so very " good to the little fishes, I do not believe " He would let their inspector suffer ship- " wreck at last:" and, " I am going on a " long journey where I think I shall see " many strange animals; but this journey " I must go alone." These and many such men have taken both birds and their eggs freely and undoubtingly, and have only loved the birds the better, and made others love them better too.

Lastly, I think I have shown you that the spirit of this teaching of Moses was far above the teaching of his own age, and many an age after. But it only received, like every other commandment of the Old Testament, its full authority and light for us in the teaching of Jesus Christ. St. Paul tells us that the whole of God's creation looks for its deliverance in Christ's coming.[1] And that is being slowly fulfilled now. Wherever the savage ferocity of past times, such as in cruel amusements, in reckless sport, or in indifference to suffering, is disappearing from amongst us, it is because we are being led higher by the spirit of the Bible and of Jesus Christ, who

[1] Rom. viii. 19.

taught us that not one sparrow falls to the ground without God's knowledge,[1] and that we, the crown of God's creation, are united with all His living creatures in the great bond of being all the family of our Father which is in heaven.

[1] St. Matt. x. 29.

# VI.

## THE GREAT QUESTION.

(Advent, 1883.)

*Almighty God, give us grace that we may cast away the works of darkness and put upon us the armour of light, now in the time of this mortal life in which thy Son Jesus Christ came to visit us in great humility: that in the last day, when he shall come again in his glorious majesty to judge both the quick and dead, we may rise to the life immortal: through him who liveth and reigneth with thee and the Holy Ghost, now and ever. Amen.*

(COLLECT FOR THE FIRST SUNDAY IN ADVENT.)

"When the Son of man cometh, shall he find faith upon the earth?"—St. Luke xviii. 8.

Last Sunday you heard of the great text of the Jewish prophet Habakkuk, "The "just shall live by his faith,"[1] and how powerfully it influenced those two very different religious reformers, St. Paul and Martin Luther. I also propose to-day to speak of the subject of faith in connection with this searching Advent question— When Christ comes again, will he or will he not find faith in us?

But what was Christ himself thinking of when he asked the question? It is very difficult to say. The words were spoken in the long talks that he had with his disciples before the last fatal journey

[1] Hab. ii. 4.

to Jerusalem. He had just told them the parable of the unjust judge, who righted the poor widow, not because it was his duty to do justice, but because he was wearied of her prayers. And if an unjust judge can be made just by unwearied prayers, "shall not God avenge his own "elect, which cry day and night unto him, "though he bear long with them? I "tell you he shall avenge them speedily. "Nevertheless when the Son of man "cometh, shall he find faith upon the "earth?"

Now this abrupt question certainly looks as if it were not a mere searching of the consciences of those who listened to his words, but a doubt in the very mind of Christ himself. A doubt in the mind of Christ himself! you may say:

did not he know all things? No; he is careful on this very subject to warn us with special solemnity that he did not. The short time of his wonderful mission was nearly over, and he was about to begin the last act of the awful tragedy. He knew that one of his own disciples meant to betray him. He knew that the boldest of his Apostles would soon deny with oaths the Master that he loved. He knew that this must end in mockery, outrage, and a cruel death. He may even have had the terrible vision before his eyes of that last moment of apparent utter failure, when he cried in despair, "My "God, my God, why hast thou forsaken "me?" And seeing all the horror to come —how very little he had been able to do as yet; how few and poor and weak his followers were, and how they must be tried — he may well have asked himself as much as them, "When the Son of "man cometh, shall he find faith upon "the earth?"

When the Son of man cometh — yes, but when will that be? Surely there is no more profound lesson in the Gospel story, none more necessary to remember if we think we honour Jesus Christ by denying the reality of his human nature, than those solemn words, "Of that day "and that hour knoweth no man, no, not "the angels which are in heaven; not even "the Son, but the Father only."[1] But he had just told them also that it should be "speedily." And they forgot the warning that even Christ himself did not know

[1] St. Mark xiii. 32.

when his coming again should be; they forgot that a thousand years in God's sight are but as one day, and remembered only that he would speedily avenge them. He had told them of a great tribulation soon to come—which was fulfilled in the famous Siege of Jerusalem under Titus in that very generation—when the terrible Romans would take their beloved city, and defile their beautiful Temple, and all the horrors of siege and famine and sack, aggravated by the fury of conquerors after a desperate resistance, would be suffered. Surely, they thought, when this trial was past, they would see their Master coming in the clouds in power and great glory. But again men's hopes grew fainter and fainter as the persecutions were renewed again and again under the worst Roman

Emperors, such as Nero and Domitian; and then the scoffers, of whom St. Peter tells us, began to say, "Where is the "promise of his coming? for since the "fathers fell asleep, all things continue "as they were from the beginning of "the creation."[1] And to some religious people even nowadays it seems, I believe, almost irreligious if you do not now believe, as the Apostles wrongly then believed, that Christ must come within a very few years.

To me it seems that the more we realise the greatness of Christ's work the less we can believe this possible. When we look on the history of the world we see that Christ's life was to us the great central point of it all. We see that the greatest

[1] 2 St. Peter iii.: 3, 4.

conquerors and statesmen who are said to have changed the faces of continents have not, all put together, changed the history of mankind as much as did this young Carpenter of Nazareth. We see that the silent influences of that work act upon those who do not believe in him—more shame to us—almost as much as on those who do, and that these influences are spreading wider every day. But on the other hand there are whole worlds of work yet left for them to do. And this being so, we may well refuse to believe that Christ's work will be ended while as yet it is utterly incomplete, or that he will willingly cease from being the Saviour of mankind while there are men who need a Saviour at all. But if any one finds that his life is made better by that belief, if he finds that he cannot watch and pray so well without it, then in God's name let him believe it. There is no difference in the warning to him and to us.

For remember that this is absolutely certain: that Christ's coming *will* to you be speedy, though he should not come to the earth for millions of ages. Young as you may be, it cannot be long before, as George Eliot says, "the commonplace, " 'we must all die' transforms itself into 'I " 'must die, and soon.'" This then is for all the Advent message, Christ is coming to me soon; what will he find the faith in me?

Now there have been, as you know, certain so-called ages of faith upon the earth, when it certainly seemed as if Christ might come suddenly and yet find faith in whole cities or whole countries. Such, for example, were the Crusades, when a single hermit preached all Europe into arms; or the Florence that you read of in *Romola*, when the whole city gave up its amusements, and took to singing litanies instead, at the preaching of the famous Savonarola.

But were these really at heart any more ages of faith than our own age? Would the hearts of Christ's people be more ready to receive Him then than now? I venture to doubt it. It seems to me that a parish or a country which goes into hysterical fits of general conversion one day, and returns to its old sins the next, is running the risk of letting the seven other devils in, and the last state is likely to be worse than the first. God forbid that we should deny whatever besetting sins there are in our own time: its over-haste to be rich; its tendency to false pretences; its failure in the simpler virtues, and so forth. But when we look on the noble efforts of thousands of good men and women for our poorer brethren in the wretched alleys of London; or the care that is shown for weak and miserable, and even utterly bad people, as compared with any other time; or the growing hatred of war, and habit of appeal to principles of justice; or the desire that every human being should have a chance of education; or the feeling for the sufferings of dumb animals: in these and a thousand other ways the influences of Christ are working, and in all these things the Son of man would find His faith in the earth.

Christ then will come to you, and soon—that is the Advent message. Year after year that message comes; does it find in us more or less faith than last year? The pulpit is not a place where any one of us would care to tell much of his inner thoughts; but at least, my friends, I cannot forget that just a year ago, on Advent Sunday, I was to have spoken to you in this Chapel, and I meant to have spoken on this very text. But God willed it otherwise. When Advent Sunday came I was stricken down by illness, and it was then possible that I should never see these faces from this pulpit again. God in His goodness, however, saw fit to give me back my health and strength; and has sent me again to deliver His message. I ask you again, as I humbly ask myself—

When the Son of man comes, will He find faith in *us* ?

In us individually, and in us as a body, for here, more than anywhere else, we are members one of another. With you, the younger generation in our public schools, as Mr. Gladstone told the boys of Winchester the other day, rests in great part the future of England. Our history here in this school, though short, has been a noble one, through the courage and the faith of our first pioneers; and with the end of this term we are coming to that serious trial for every public school—the loss of the head-master, whose firm, wise lead we have heartily followed. Let us pray that Haileybury may be guided in the future as it has been in the past, religiously, yet without the cheap parade of religion ; so strong in faith that we can afford to be gentle to those who are weaker. Let us resolve this Advent resolutely to cast away those works of darkness that from time to time have sullied our name, and make it our earnest endeavour that we may send forth (as the Bidding Prayer puts it) *a due supply of persons qualified to serve God in Church and State;* and that each of these may in his own degree be helping to make the waste places of the world again into a garden of the Lord.

And lastly, to each of us individually also is this question put. For you may, by habit, or discipline, or example, be leading a blameless and wholesome life, and it will be the faith of Christ, for the most part, that has made such a life easy for you. But if you have not the faith *in* you, there is nothing else that can lift you into the higher life. "Without faith it is *im-* "*possible* to please God."[1] He who fights strongly for what he believes to be true, and is loyal to it whether others laugh at him or not, has the precious gift of faith, whether his faith be right or wrong; he has not yet received the promises, but has seen them afar off, and is persuaded of them, and embraces them, and confesses that he is a stranger and pilgrim on the earth.[2] For, in the beautiful words of the greatest teacher of our own day,[3] "If loving "well the creatures that are like yourself, "you feel that you would love still more "dearly creatures that are better than "yourself, were they revealed to you; if "striving with all your might to mend

---

[1] Heb. xi. 6.      [2] Heb. xi. 13.
[3] Ruskin: *The Bible of Amiens*, Part IV.

"what is evil, near you and around, you
"would fain look for a day when some
"Judge of all the earth shall wholly do
"right, and the little hills rejoice on every
"side; if parting with the companions
"that have given you all the best joy you
"had on earth, you desire ever to meet
"their eyes again and to clasp their hands,
"where eyes shall no more be dim nor
"hands fail; if preparing yourself to lie
"down beneath the grass in silence and
"loneliness, seeing no more beauty and
"feeling no more gladness, you would care
"for the promise of a time when you
"should see God's light again, and know
"the things you have longed to know,
"and walk in the peace of everlasting
"Love—then the Hope of these things to
"you is Religion, the Substance of them

" in your life is Faith. And in the power
" of them it is promised us that the king-
" doms of this world shall yet become
" the kingdoms of our Lord and of His
" Christ."

# VII.

## HEAVEN.

(November 1885.)

*O God, whose blessed Son was manifested that he might destroy the works of the devil, and make us the sons of God and heirs of eternal life: Grant us, we beseech thee, that having this hope we may purify ourselves even as he is pure; that when he shall appear again with power and great glory we may be made like unto him in his eternal and glorious kingdom, where with thee, O Father, and thee, O Holy Ghost, he liveth and reigneth, one God, world without end. Amen.*

(COLLECT FOR THE SIXTH SUNDAY AFTER EPIPHANY.)

> "And the streets of the city shall be full of boys and girls playing in the streets thereof."—ZECHARIAH viii. 5.

SOME children-friends of mine were at a children's service not long ago. They did not remember much of the sermon, but they evidently had been struck by this text, which is indeed a remarkable one. The beautiful vision of happy children playing in the streets of God's own city is indeed so unlike what we generally associate with the stern and grim old prophets of the Jews, that I resolved myself to choose it for the subject of my next sermon, and try to explain the vision to you.

What is this city in which the streets shall be full of playing boys and girls? It is Jerusalem—but a Jerusalem that never existed at all, except in the Prophet's mind. But in order to understand what he was now dreaming of you must listen first to what was happening in his time.

Zechariah was the son of a priest, and was born at Babylon during the time when the poor Jewish captives who had been torn from their homes used to hang their harps on the willows by the hated river Euphrates, when they thought of Jerusalem and the ruined Temple on Mount Zion, to which there seemed no hope of return. At last arose the great King Cyrus, who made the Persians instead of the Medes the most powerful race in his empire—the same king whose boyhood and education many of you have read about in the earliest historical romance in the world, the *Cyropaedia* of Xenophon. Now in the very first year that King Cyrus came to the throne and found himself with almost absolute power to do as he pleased, he issued an edict, which turned out in its remoter consequences to be one of the most important in history, though no doubt he himself thought it was only an act of generosity, befitting a young king coming to the throne, to a handful of harmless exiles. This is what the Book of Chronicles says, "The "Lord stirred up the spirit of Cyrus king "of Persia, that he made a proclamation "throughout all his kingdom, and also put "it in writing, saying, Thus saith Cyrus "king of Persia, All the kingdoms of the "earth hath the God of heaven given me; "and he hath charged me to build him an "house in Jerusalem. Who is there among "you of all his people? The Lord his God "be with him, and let him go up."[1] A caravan of exiles therefore returned with hope and delight under the commander Zerubbabel, the high priest Joshua, and the prophets Haggai and Zechariah. They pictured to themselves, no doubt, the house of God revived in greater glory than even the Temple of Solomon, and the voice of prayer and praise arising from the people gathered on the holy mountain. But how very seldom do the realities of things come up to our hopes! Even as they stood in the blackened ruins of the city, with gaunt rubbish-heaps marking where the Temple had stood, they must have felt their hearts sinking, and their fears were only too soon to be realised.

But I need not stop to say anything

---

[1] 2 Chron. xxxvi. 22.

about the history of that period, interesting as it is—how the Samaritans first tried to join them, and then being rejected did all they could to hinder them; how the supplies of stone and timber were often stopped, or the wages of the workmen were stolen during the carriage from Persia ; how fine houses began to be built at Jerusalem, apparently with the cedar and marble and ivory that had been sent for the house of God ;[1] until at length Cyrus was dead, and his mad son Cambyses too, and also the impostor who pretended to be the murdered Prince Smerdis: so that it was not until the reign of Darius, twenty years later, that, thanks in part to his finding the half-forgotten decree of Cyrus in the archives at Ecbatana,[2] the

---

[1] Haggai i. 4.  [2] Ezra vi. 1.

work at length was really finished. That the work was ever finished at all was due not so much to Zerubbabel, the general, or to Joshua, the high priest, or all the other priests together, as it was to those two prophets of the Return, the aged Haggai and the young Zechariah. Time after time when the Jews' hearts failed them did these two prophets inspire them with fresh enthusiasm, and Zechariah, the younger and more eager of the two, is never tired of dwelling, not on their present troubles, but on the happiness and peace that were sure to come. And in answer to those who argued that all these trials were signs of God's anger, and that they ought to fast and mourn to please Him, he answers in splendid words, that remind us of Isaiah, the greatest of the prophets:

"Thus saith the Lord, When ye fasted and mourned all these years, did ye fast to me? Thus speaketh the Lord, Execute true judgment, and show mercy and compassion every man to his brother, and let none imagine evil against his brother in his heart. For the Lord saith: I am returned to Zion, and will dwell in the midst of Jerusalem: and Jerusalem shall be called a city of truth; and the mountain of the Lord shall be called the holy mountain. And the streets of the city shall be full of boys and girls playing in the streets thereof."

Alas! as I said, this city never existed at all except in the prophet's mind. The new city and the new Temple rose up, it is true, in revived beauty, and the people dwelt there safely again. Once more the tribes came up thither year by year to worship God on the holy mountain. But the perfect purity, justice, and happiness of which he dreamed were not to be found in any city—never will be found in any city so long as the world lasts. And so four hundred years later the Temple again was taken, and the streets of Jerusalem were running red with the blood of the boys and girls who had played in them.

But what of that? Because the prophets only saw as it were in a glass darkly, does that make their visions of no value to us? Look at the greatest instance of all. In a few weeks we shall be keeping the birthday of that Saviour whose coming all the prophets foretold. Not one of them ever dreamed of anything but a great conquering King and Lawgiver, under whom all enemies would be beaten down, and the land rejoice under the shadow of his sceptre. How very different was the form in which the Saviour came—the humble Carpenter of Nazareth, who was crucified like a slave outside the Prophet's own city. But that will not, I trust, prevent us next Christmas morning from entering into the spirit of that grand first lesson, "Unto us a child is born, unto us "a son is given: and the government shall "be upon his shoulder: and his name shall "be called Wonderful, Counsellor, The "mighty God, The everlasting Father, "The Prince of Peace."[1]

It is not therefore needful that the prophecy should have been fulfilled, for us to enter heart and soul into the Prophet's

[1] Isaiah ix. 6.

beautiful vision; nor is there anything more likely than such a vision to lift us into a purer and brighter world than what we really see around us. Is there anybody indeed, boy or girl, or woman or man, who does not have a dream of Heaven at times? In that pathetic book, *Misunderstood*, which I was reading to some of you lately, there is a sentence about the sermon which came to my mind when I thought over this text. "Humphrey
" did not often listen to the sermon, but
" to-day it was all about Heaven, and he
" liked to hear about Heaven, because his
" mother was there. Feeble must human
" language ever be to paint the glories
" of that far-off land, but were not one
" and all bound to the land the preacher
" was describing? And was there one

"there who could say, What is this
"to me?"

Ah, my friends, is it true that we are all bound to the Happy City? Is it true that we all not only would like to see it realised, but will do our part, God helping us, to make it possible? For unless we do more than wish, unless we do our part each one, be it but the carrying of a brick for the work, be sure that for us God's City will never be built.

Take the text once more, and see what it is that the Prophet requires. "The "streets of the city shall be full of boys "and girls playing in the streets thereof."

The first thing then that we notice is the perfect *peace and security*. No boys or girls can be playing in the streets of a town where robbers and murderers are about within, or where the foe are shooting their arrows from without. But why is one city ever in danger from another? "From whence come wars and fightings "amongst you? Come they not hence, "even of your lusts that war in your "members? Ye lust and have not: ye "kill, and desire to have: ye fight and "war, yet ye have not."[1] Therefore, to make the Happy City there must be Justice within and without; no man shall spoil his neighbour's goods; the weaker shall not fear the stronger.

Secondly, if the boys and girls are to play in the streets, the desire of Gain cannot have eaten up the whole heart of the City. No one is so foolish as to look on the trade and commerce of a great city

[1] St. James iv. 1, 2.

as a sin, with all the far-reaching opportunities that this gives for noble as well as for base uses. A city does well to pride itself upon its stately buildings, its well-stocked markets, its busy harbour filled with a forest of masts and sails from distant lands. But when, as one is often forced to believe, Gain is the one object of a city's desire, to which everything else is to be sacrificed, then surely that is a demon that is worshipped, and not the true spring of human industry. This it is that covered Niagara with advertisements of soap and pills; that stole half the commons of England from the poor; that choked our rivers with poison, and our valleys with slag; that let little children rot away in mines; and that created those miles upon miles of dismal streets in the north, where the sun never shines through the heavy vapour, and if the boys and girls ever play at all it must be upon ash-heaps. Assuredly Gain will not be the greatest aim of life in the Happy City. In the famous city of Amsterdam, itself one of the greatest commercial towns in Europe, there still exists a curious custom. In the year 1622, when the cruel Spaniards were trying to crush the Netherlands, and stamp out their freedom and their faith, some children, it is said, discovered a plot to take the city. Ever since then, on the first week of the *Kermes* or fair, the Great Exchange, where grave merchants ordinarily meet for business, is entirely given up to the boys and girls of the town to play in. I could fancy Zechariah looking on at this, and thinking that part of his vision had already become true.

Thirdly, in the heavenly vision notice that not only are there boys and girls, but that they are *playing*, without the Prophet thinking it wrong or foolish of them to do so. The real Heaven and the real heavenly things are not, you see, only for older people when they are getting tired of this world; the boys and girls have their place too, and it is a place they may well wish for at once. What can be sadder than that a child should ever be taught anything else? The dreary Sabbaths, with wholesome exercise for body and mind alike forbidden, the long dull services and sermons, and the wholly unnatural notion of goodness that once used to be common, are now, thank God, very rare in England. Most people would now see that to tell a boy, as one of the old hymn-writers does, that Heaven is a place

> "Where congregations ne'er break up,
> And Sabbaths never end,"

is the surest way, if he is a spirited English boy, to make him resolve that he will never run the risk of being sent to Heaven. But show him that the Heaven which the Bible tells of is a place where you are always kind and just to others, because others are always kind and just to you; show him that the many perplexities and temptations of a boy's life are cleared and smoothed for him by a love greater than that of his father and mother; show him, above all, that to be fitted for this Heaven he must *not* be a hypocrite or unnatural at all, but that God loves play in its place, so long as it is kindly and healthy and innocent, just as much as He loves honest work—and then it is hard if you do not get that boy in his better moments to resolve that he too will make a push for the land that is very far off.

Fourthly and lastly, there is something, perhaps, in the mention of the boys and girls together, which seems to speak of the remaining condition for the happy children—that they must be pure and innocent in their play. Without that there will be no happiness in their play, you may be sure. With that, it is better that boys and girls should be together at times, each learning something from the other. A girl is better off who has brothers, and a boy is better off who has sisters. She learns that boys are not necessarily the rough rude creatures that foolish people often imagine, and so encourage them to be, but are generous in proportion as they are manly; and he learns that girls are not unfitted to be his companions, but make him better by their gentler and purer minds, and by calling out that protecting instinct of the stronger towards the weaker, which is strongest in the most generous heart.

Thus then we see that all the Prophet required to make the Happy City of the boys and girls was Justice, Unselfishness, Sympathy, and Innocence. Surely these need no magic. These need not, like the gates of pearl or the glassy sea, the white-robed harpers or the golden crowns, seem only the distant vision of a dream. The question for you is, Do you really desire these things? for if you do, you will have them. But, like the Jews with Zechariah, you will often find your hopes disappointed: the Happy City will not be built at once—it will not be built indeed in all its glory while this world lasts. But if you really desire Justice, Unselfishness, Sympathy, and Innocence, you will yet see rising—ay, even here in a great English public school—the walls of that New Jerusalem that prophets and all good men have longed for; and each one of you, as an honest, manly, kindly English schoolboy will be really doing his part to build up the Eternal City of God.

THE END.

*Printed by* R. & R. CLARK, *Edinburgh*.

www.ingramcontent.com/pod-product-compliance
Lightning Source LLC
Chambersburg PA
CBHW020100170426
43199CB00009B/353